First
Nature
Book

First Nature Book

Robert Wellesley

TREASURE PRESS

The world of nature

Nature means everything in the world which human beings have not made. Nature includes rocks, the earth, weather, rivers and the oceans, but usually we think of Nature as being about animals and plants. These are the parts of Nature that interest most people.

Animals and plants are the two kinds of living things. Nearly all animals can move about, but most plants are fixed in one place. All animals eat plants or other animals, but most plants produce their own food.

Plants

Plants are found all over the world. Some are so small that you can only see them with the help of a microscope. Many of these microscopic plants live in the sea. Seaweeds are a kind of plant, called algae. They are very simple plants, and they do not have flowers. Mosses and ferns are also plants that do not have flowers. Fungi are a special sort of plant. They cannot make their own food. Instead, they get food from dead plants and animals.

The plants we know best are the flowering plants. These include grasses, vegetables, garden and countryside flowers, and most trees. The flowers produce seeds. Some trees, like the pines and spruces, are not flowering plants. They produce seeds in cones.

The main parts of a flowering plant are the roots, stem and leaves. Roots grow in the soil. They anchor the plant to the ground. They also take up water and minerals from the soil. A plant needs water and minerals so that it can grow. The stem grows up towards the sun. It has to be strong enough to support the rest of the plant. The leaves are usually thin and flat. Their job is to make the plant's food. Leaves are green because they contain a substance called chlorophyll. Chlorophyll absorbs energy from the sun, and uses it to make sugar from water and carbon dioxide (a gas found in the air).

A flower produces seeds. The seeds only grow if pollen has been brought from another flower. This is called pollination. Pollen is carried from one plant to another by the wind, or by insects like bees and butterflies. Insects are attracted to the flowers by the bright colours of the petals. They feed on the nectar at the bottom of the flower.

The seeds of the plant grow in a fruit. A wheat grain is a fruit which contains one seed. Apples and blackberries are fruits with many seeds. When the fruits are ripe, they fall to the ground. The seeds grow into new plants.

Flowering plants come in all shapes and sizes. Some plants live for only one year. They are called annuals. Annuals grow from a seed, then flower and die between spring and autumn. Other plants live for a long time. They are called perennials. Some, like the narcissus, grow from a bulb. The bulb is a store of food. The leaves and stem grow from it. After the flower has died, the leaves wither and die, but the bulb remains alive.

Trees are large plants with big stems, called trunks. The trunk of a tree is made of wood. It is strong enough to support a huge number of leaves and branches. The wood is protected by a layer of bark. As the tree grows, its trunk gets bigger. When the tree is cut down, you can tell how old it is by counting the rings in its trunk. Some trees shed their leaves in autumn. They are called deciduous trees. Other trees keep their leaves all the year. They are called evergreens.

Animals

There are two main kinds of animals: vertebrates and invertebrates. Animals without backbones are called invertebrates. Sponges, jellyfish and sea anemones are invertebrates with soft bodies. Snails, cowries, cockles and mussels have soft bodies, which are protected by hard shells. They are called molluscs. Octopuses and squid are molluscs without hard shells. Other invertebrates have a hard outer skeleton, like a suit of armour. They include the insects (which have three pairs of legs), the spiders (which have four pairs of legs), and the crabs and lobsters (which have five pairs of legs).

There are more kinds of insects than
any other sort of animal. Their bodies
have three parts. The head carries
the antennae, or feelers. The thorax bears
the legs and wings. The abdomen is the third and largest part.

The lives of many insects are divided into four parts. Butterflies, moths, bees
and flies live like this. First the egg is laid. This hatches and out comes
a caterpillar, or grub, which eats as much as it can. Then the caterpillar
hides somewhere, and becomes a pupa in a hard case. The pupa of a butterfly
is called a chrysalis. Moths spin a cocoon of silk, which hides the pupa.
The cocoons of the silk moth are used to make silk cloth.
Some time later, the pupa case opens and
the adult insect comes out.

Other insects do not go through these stages. They look almost like the adult insect as soon as they hatch out from the egg. They are called nymphs. Nymphs do not have wings.

The second large group of animals are the vertebrates. Human beings and all the big animals are vertebrates. They all have backbones.

Fishes are vertebrates which live in water. Their bodies are covered with scales. They swim with their fins, and breathe through gills. Amphibians, like the toads, frogs and newts, spend part of their lives on land and part in the water. Baby amphibians are called tadpoles. They have gills. When they become adult, they grow lungs. The eggs of amphibians are called spawn.

Reptiles have bodies which are covered in scales. They lay their eggs on land. Lizards are very common reptiles. Snakes have lost their legs, and crawl on their bellies. Crocodiles and alligators live in rivers. Tortoises and turtles are protected by a thick shell. The dinosaurs were huge reptiles which died out, or became extinct, 130 million years ago.

Birds are flying animals. Their front legs have turned into wings, and their bodies are covered with feathers which keep them warm. A bird has no hands. It uses its beak to pick up food and to make its nest. The bird lays its eggs in the nest. The parents sit on the eggs to keep them warm until they are ready to hatch. This is called incubating the eggs. Some baby birds, or chicks, stay in the nest until they learn to fly. Other chicks can leave the nest and run about soon after they hatch. Male birds sing to tell other males to keep away, and to attract females. Some birds cannot fly. Penguins use their wings, or flippers, for swimming instead of flying. Ostriches cannot fly, but they have strong legs for running.

Mammals are animals which have a coat of hair or fur. They are warm-blooded, which means that their bodies stay at the same temperature all the time. Birds are warm-blooded, too. The fur helps mammals to keep warm. Human beings are mammals. We have clothes instead of fur to keep us warm. Nearly all mammals give birth to babies. Only two, the duck-billed platypus and the echidna of Australia, lay eggs. Baby mammals are fed on their mother's milk until they are old enough to eat solid food. Baby cats and mice are naked and helpless when they are born. Their eyes do not open for several days, and they do not start to walk for some time. Baby deer and horses can stand, and even run, when they are only a few hours old. They have to follow their mothers while they search for grass to eat.

Most of the animals we keep as pets are mammals. So are farmyard animals, and the animals we see at the zoo. Horses, cattle, sheep, deer and antelopes have hooves and are good runners. Dogs and cats are meat-eating hunters. Their wild relations are wolves, lions and tigers. Bats are mammals which fly like birds. They usually come out at night to hunt insects. Whales are mammals which live in the sea and swim like fish. Their tails have flat flukes, which act like the fins of a fish. Whales have no hair. They are kept warm by a thick layer of fat, called blubber, under their skin. Elephants, rhinoceroses and hippopotamuses also have bare skin, to help them keep cool. Monkeys have tails. Most of them live in trees. The chimpanzee, gorilla, orang-utan and the gibbons are all apes. They do not have tails.

All animals are related to each other. They are descended from a single ancestor which lived hundreds of millions of years ago. Since then, animals have gradually changed shape, and new kinds of animals have been formed. This gradual change is called evolution. Closely related animals look like one another. Monkeys and apes are our close relations, so they look like us. Insects do not look like us, and they are very, very distantly related. People often gave names to animals before they knew how they were related. Starfish were given their name because they live in the sea, and they have five arms like the points of a star. Yet starfish are not really related to fish. This is just a name. Seahorses are not horses. They are fish. So we must not think that two animals are nearly the same, just because they have the same kind of name.

The way plants and animals live

Plants can live anywhere in the world where they can find water and the minerals which they need to grow. They can make their food if sunlight falls on their leaves. Animals can live only where there are plants. They need plants to get energy. Some animals do not eat plants, but they eat other animals that feed on plants. So, in the end, the food of all animals comes from plants. The fox is a meat-eater. It eats rabbits. Rabbits eat grass. This is called a food chain.

People sometimes think that animals are free to go wherever they please. They say 'as free as a bird'. But an animal must stay where it can find its proper food. A fox must live near rabbits. An animal must also have shelter, where it can sleep in safety, and where it can bring up its babies. The place where an animal lives is called its habitat. Each kind of animal has its own kind of habitat, which supplies it with everything it needs in life. A duck's habitat is a pond, where it finds water plants and small animals to eat. The duck makes its nest among the tall plants which grow at the edge of the pond. The eggs will be safe from enemies. When the eggs hatch, the duck can take her ducklings for a swim.

Plants have habitats, too. The cactus lives in the desert. Very little rain falls in the desert, so a cactus has to save its water. It stores water in its thick stem. Other plants need plenty of water. They live in wet places. Some plants even live in ponds and rivers. Mistletoe has a very special habitat. It grows on another tree. Mistletoe gets its water and minerals from the tree.

A zoologist is a person who studies animals. A botanist studies plants. Zoologists and botanists are interested in how animals live. They want to know how each one forms a link in a food chain, and what is its habitat. As towns get bigger and more countryside is turned into farmland, there is less room for wild animals and plants. Poisons from factories kill them. Zoologists and botanists study food chains and habitats, so that they can try to save wild things. Saving wild animals and plants and preventing the destruction of their habitats is called conservation. You can help with conservation if you do not disturb animals or pick flowers, especially if they are rare.

Aa

Acorn

The acorn is the fruit of the oak tree. It is an
oval nut seated in a cup. The cup of this turkey oak
is covered with long 'fur'. In past times acorns
were used to feed pigs and cattle. They were also
ground into flour to make bread. The corks used
in bottles are made from the bark of the cork oak,
which grows in Spain and Portugal.

Albatross

Albatrosses are large seabirds. They are found
mainly in seas south of the Equator. They have
long, slender wings, sometimes as long as 3.5 metres.
Albatrosses can fly for very long distances
over the sea with hardly a beat of their wings.
Our picture shows a black-browed albatross.
It has a patch of black feathers over each eye.

Alligator

The alligator is very like a crocodile. It lives
in the warm rivers of North America and China.
When an alligator closes its mouth, all its teeth
are hidden. The mother alligator lays her eggs
in a nest on the river bank. Sometimes she lays
as many as 80 eggs. Alligators eat fishes and
land animals which come to the water's edge to drink.

Ant

Ants are small insects with six legs and a pair of antennae. They use their antennae to feel their way about, and to smell with. Ants live in large groups, called colonies. The queen ant lays lots of eggs. The eggs develop into white pupae, which you can see in the picture. From these hatch the males and the future queens, as well as the worker ants. The workers are females which cannot lay eggs, and which do not have wings. There are 8,000 different kinds of ants.

Antelope

Antelopes belong to the cattle family. Usually only the males have horns.
There are many kinds of antelopes in Africa, and a few in Asia. Some antelopes are no bigger than rabbits, others are as big as a bull.

Bb

Baboon

Baboons are large African monkeys. They live in family parties, called troops. In the daytime they feed on the ground. At night they sleep in the trees. Baboons eat all kinds of plants and small animals. If they are attacked by an enemy, the male baboons fight fiercely to defend the mothers and babies. The picture shows a family of yellow baboons.

Badger

Badgers live in woods. They are stocky and look like small bears. Their front feet have strong claws for digging. Badgers eat earthworms, insects, frogs, bulbs and berries. They live in burrows, and come out at night to feed. Badgers in Europe are grey, with black and white stripes on their heads. American badgers have narrower, white stripes on their faces.

Bat

Bats are the only mammals which fly properly, like birds. A bat is able to fly because it has very long arms and fingerbones, which have a web of skin stretched across them. It also has strong shoulder muscles, which beat these wings. Bats live throughout most of the world. Some feed on insects, some feed on fruit. The bat in the picture is a fruit bat.
When they sleep, bats hang upside down. Look at the bat in the picture. It is holding on to the tree with the long claws on its hindfeet.

Bear

Bears are the biggest and strongest meat-eaters
in the world. They live in wild mountainous country
and in forests. Although they look so big, bears usually
do no harm unless they are wounded, or unless they are
protecting their babies.

Beaver

A beaver is a large
rodent, or gnawing
animal, which lives in
rivers in North America,
Europe and Asia.
It has a flat, scaly tail
and waterproof fur.
A pair of beavers build
a dam, made of branches

Bee

and mud. The dam holds back the water to form a pond. In the pond the beavers build their home, or lodge, with sticks.

Bees are hairy flying insects. They feed on the nectar and pollen of flowers. Bees store food in the form of honey. They live in large groups, or colonies. There is only one queen bee in the colony. She lays all the eggs. From the eggs hatch grubs, or larvae, which the workers feed with honey. The grubs turn into pupae, which hatch into bees.

Beetle

There are thousands of different kinds of beetles. They live all over the world.
Beetles have one pair of flying wings, and also another pair of wings
that have hardened to form wing cases. When the beetle is resting, the wing cases
close over to protect the flying wings. You can see this in the picture.
Some beetles are pests. They spoil trees or food crops. The picture shows
a beautiful beetle from South Africa laying its eggs.

Birch

Birch trees are found in cool, northern lands, like Britain. They usually grow
on heaths or moors, or on the sides of mountains. The best-known birch in Europe
is the silver birch in the picture. It has a silvery white trunk and slender branches
which sway gracefully in the wind.

Blackbird

Only the male blackbird is black. He has a yellow bill. The hen blackbird
is brown and she has a brown bill. Blackbirds eat earthworms, insects and berries.
They have a lovely song. Blackbirds build a cup-shaped nest, which is made of grass,
leaves, moss or wool. They line the nest first with mud, and then with grass.

Bluebell

The bluebell is a flower of the Lily family. It grows in Europe. It has sword-shaped leaves, and blue flowers shaped like bells. A bluebell grows from a swollen underground bulb. Bluebells die very quickly if you pick them.

Bushbaby

Bushbabies get their name because their call is like a baby crying. They live in the hot, wet forests of Africa. Bushbabies have large, staring eyes and large ears. You can see how their hands and feet grasp the branches as they jump from tree to tree. Their grey fur is very soft, and their tails are very long and bushy.

Butterfly

Most butterflies have lovely coloured wings. Some are very beautiful indeed. A butterfly's wings are covered with tiny coloured scales which form different patterns. Usually butterflies fly about in the daytime. A butterfly folds its wings together over its back when it is resting. There are many different kinds of butterfly. They live all over the world. The largest and most colourful live in the tropical jungles.

Below: tiger swallowtail butterfly. Above right: mountain blue swallowtail butterfly. Below right: peacock butterfly.

Cactus

The cactus is a plant which lives in the desert,
where there is very little rain. It stores water
in its stems. You can see the stems in the picture.
They are swollen and green. The leaves are no more
than prickles. Most plants lose moisture through
their leaves. Because it has such tiny leaves,
a cactus does not lose any water.

Camel

There are two kinds of camel. The camels in the picture have only one hump.
They live in North Africa. The other kind of camel has two humps, and lives in Asia.
The camel's humps contain fat, so it does not need to eat very often. It can
also go for a long time without drinking.

Cat

People first started to keep cats five thousand years ago in Ancient Egypt.
They kept cats because the cats caught mice and rats. Cats still do this, but now
people usually keep them as pets. At first the tabby cat was the most common cat.
Now there are many other colours and breeds. Above: blue spotted tabby.
Right: tabby and white kitten. Following page left: two Siamese cats.
Following page right: long-haired chinchilla cat.

Caterpillar

Caterpillars are the grubs, or larvae,
which hatch out from the eggs
of butterflies and moths. A caterpillar
does not look anything like the insect
it will finally become. Its body
is divided into rings. The first three
of these rings each carry a pair
of tiny legs. As it grows, the caterpillar
sheds its old skin, and grows a new one.
Then it turns into a pupa, or chrysalis.
Finally, the perfect butterfly or moth
comes out of the chrysalis.

Catkin

Catkins are the flowers of certain trees,
such as the birch, hazel and alder.
They open in the spring, when
the leaves on the tree are beginning
to unfold. A popular name for catkins
is 'lambs' tails'. There are male catkins
and female catkins. During the summer,
the female catkins change to form
the fruits of the tree. Sometimes
these are nuts, sometimes cones.
The nuts or cones contain the seeds
of the tree.

Chameleon

Chameleons are tree lizards. Most of them live
in Africa. Unlike most lizards, they move
very slowly. When chameleons are alarmed,
they stay very still so that
their green or brown colouring blends with
the colours of the tree. It is not true
that chameleons can change colour to suit
any background. They do, however, change colour
with the intensity of light, or when
they are angry. Chameleons have fingers and toes
which grasp the branches of the tree.
They shoot out their long tongues to catch insects.

Cheetah

The cheetah is a member of the cat family. It is one of the fastest animals on land. The cheetah has a long slim body and long legs. Its fur is usually reddish with black spots, and it has stripes on its tail and face.
Most cheetahs live in Africa. Once they were very common in India. They were trained for hunting by the Indian princes.

Chimpanzee

The chimpanzee is an ape. It is supposed to be more like a man than any
other animal. It has long, coarse, black hair, except on its face, hands and feet.
Chimpanzees live in family parties in the hot rain forests of Africa. They feed
mainly on fruit. The mother chimpanzee looks after her baby very lovingly.

Clam

The clam is a sea animal. It has a soft body, which is protected by hard shells.
When it is disturbed, the clam shuts the shells together. Some clams
can jump by suddenly slapping the shells together. Other clams are fixed
to rocks by strong threads. The picture shows a giant clam. It measures
1 metre across and weighs 250 kilograms.

Cobra

Cobras are poisonous snakes. They live in hot countries.
Their poison is so strong that it can kill a man.
The cobra has a sort of hood behind its neck.
When it is alarmed, it rears up and its hood swells out.
This makes the snake look very frightening.

Coral

Corals live in the sea. Each coral
is made up of a mass of tiny animals,
called polyps.When the polyps die,
their skeletons remain underneath
the living coral. Some corals are hard
with chalky skeletons. These corals
build large coral reefs. Other corals
are soft corals, like the sea fan
in the picture.

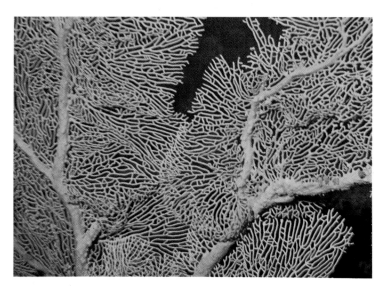

Cow

Thousands of years ago, huge, wild cattle with long, fearsome horns
roamed through the forests of Europe. The men living then hunted these cattle
for their meat. One day, someone caught a young cow, or calf, and tamed it.
Other calves were caught and kept by men. Today cows give us fresh milk.
The young bulls are killed to give us meat.

Cowrie

The cowrie is a kind of sea snail. The coils of
the shell which you see in most sea snails are hidden
inside the cowrie, so that its shell looks oval.
Cowries were once used as money in some parts
of the world. They were also collected because
they were so beautiful. So in many places today
cowries are now becoming rare. In the picture
you can see a tiger cowrie. The edges of its
fleshy mantle cover the lower part of the shell.
It is crawling over a coral.

Crab

In the sea there are many animals which wear a coat
of armour. Their legs, as well as their bodies,
are covered in this armour. They also have claws, which
they use to catch their food and to defend themselves
from their enemies. Some of these animals are called
lobsters, others are called shrimps. There are also
some with rounded bodies, which are called crabs.
There are many different crabs. They live all over
the world. When they walk, they look very funny,
because they walk sideways.

Crane

The crane is a large bird, with long legs and a long neck. Cranes live in many different parts of the world. This crowned crane lives in Africa. It has a beautiful dance, which you can see in the picture.

Crocodile

There are many different crocodiles. The largest crocodile lives in the rivers of northern Australia. It can be as large as 6.5 metres long. The smallest crocodile lives in West Africa. It is only 1 metre long. Other crocodiles live in warm rivers in southern Asia, Africa and South America. Crocodiles are reptiles. They have scaly skins. Crocodiles lay eggs. The baby crocodiles are very small when they hatch. The female crocodile builds a nest for the eggs and guards them carefully.

Cuckoo

Most female cuckoos lay their eggs in other birds' nests. So the mother cuckoo does not need to make a nest or look after her babies herself. The common cuckoo spends the winter in Africa. In the spring it flies north to Europe to breed. Only the male makes the familiar 'cuckoo' call. The cuckoo shown in the picture lives in New Zealand. It flies over 3,200 kilometres to spend the winter in the Solomon Islands.

38

Dd

Dandelion

The dandelion is a common wild plant. Its name comes
from the French words *dents de lion*, which mean lion's teeth.
If you look at the leaves of a dandelion, you will see why.
The dandelion has bright yellow flowers. Each flower
is made up of many small flowers, called florets.
When each floret is dead, a seed appears. The seed has an
umbrella of down, so it can be carried along on the wind.

Deer

Deer are shy, dainty animals. Most deer have brown coats. They often live
in the woods, but they come out into the fields at night to eat grass.
The picture shows a baby deer. It is called a fawn. Fawns have white spots
on their brown coats. We say they are dappled. When they lie down
among the bushes, they are very hard to see.

40

Dog

Dogs have been with us for a very long time.
Prehistoric man had dogs 10,000 years ago.
Dogs are very popular pets, because they are
very friendly and you can train them.
The dogs we know today are descended from
wild wolves. Now there are many different
kinds of dogs. You can see some of them
in the pictures. Below: old English sheepdog.
Above right: curly-coated retriever. Below
right: Hungarian vizsla. Far right: borzoi.

Dolphin

Dolphins are small whales. They are very friendly
and intelligent, and they can be taught to do tricks.
When dolphins are free, they live in the seas in groups,
called schools. Although dolphins live in the water,
they have to come up to the surface to breathe air.

Donkey

Donkeys are often kept as pets. In some countries
they are used to carry loads. All donkeys have
long ears. Most of them have a mane of hair
on their necks, and most donkeys have coarse brown fur
with a dark cross on their backs. The donkey is
a very patient animal, not stupid as some people think.

44

Dragonfly

When you go for a walk by the side of a river on a sunny day, look out for a brightly coloured insect darting over the water. It has a long body and two pairs of wings, which look like gauze. This is the dragonfly, or mosquito hawk, as it is called in North America. It feeds on smaller insects, which it catches in the air. The beautiful dragonfly in the picture lives in South Africa.

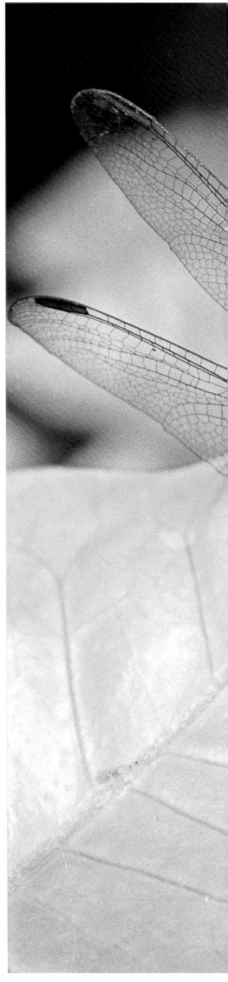

Duck

There are very many kinds of duck all over the world. They always live on or near water. The male duck, called a drake, is usually more brightly coloured than the female duck. Some ducks feed on the surface of the water. Some dabble in the water for plants or insects. Some dive completely under the water for their food. The mallard is one of the best known of the wild ducks. Many ducks are kept on ornamental ponds. One of these is the northern pintail duck, which is shown in the picture.

Ee

Eagle

Eagles are birds of prey. They feed on other birds
and small mammals. They seize their prey in their strong claws
and tear the flesh with their hooked beaks. The golden eagle
shown in the picture is one of the largest and strongest eagles.
It is often called the King of Birds. It lives high up
in the mountains. An eagle's nest is called an eyrie.

Earwig

The earwig is an insect. It has a long body, with a pair of pincers at the end. Earwigs have large wings, but we seldom see them because they are hidden, neatly folded under the small wing covers. Earwigs feed on plants and on other insects, such as plant lice.

Elephant

The elephant is the largest of all the land animals. It is very heavy, and it has thick legs like pillars to support its weight. There are two kinds of elephant. One lives in Africa, the other lives in Asia. Both have long, white tusks, which are made of very hard bone, called ivory. Elephants also have long trunks, which they use to carry food and water to their mouths. They eat leaves, branches of trees, grass and fruit. Elephants live in herds.

Elm

Elms are tall trees. Their leaves have
toothed edges. Each of their seeds
is surrounded by a leafy wing, so that
the seeds can be carried by the wind.
Elm wood lasts a long time in water. It was
once used to build bridges and wharves.
Drainpipes, buried in the ground,
also used to be made of elm wood.
Many elm trees have been killed by
Dutch Elm disease, which is carried
by beetles.

Eucalyptus

Eucalyptus trees are tall trees
which grow in Australia.
They are also called gum trees.
The trunks and branches
of eucalyptus trees have
a smooth, grey bark. The leaves
are long and narrow,
and the flowers are small,
either creamy-white or red.
Eucalyptus trees have
a strong smell. The leaves
produce an oil which is used
in medicines.

Ff

Falcon

Falcons are birds of prey. They fly very fast to hunt the small birds which they eat. They catch them with sharp, curved claws, called talons. Falcons have a hooked beak, which they use to tear the flesh. Before guns were invented, men used to hunt birds with trained falcons.

Fir tree

Firs are tall trees with straight trunks. Their branches grow straight out sideways. Their leaves are small, stiff and narrow, and are called needles. Fir trees have no flowers. Their seeds are in the brown cones which grow on the branches. Firs keep their leaves in winter, so they are called evergreen.

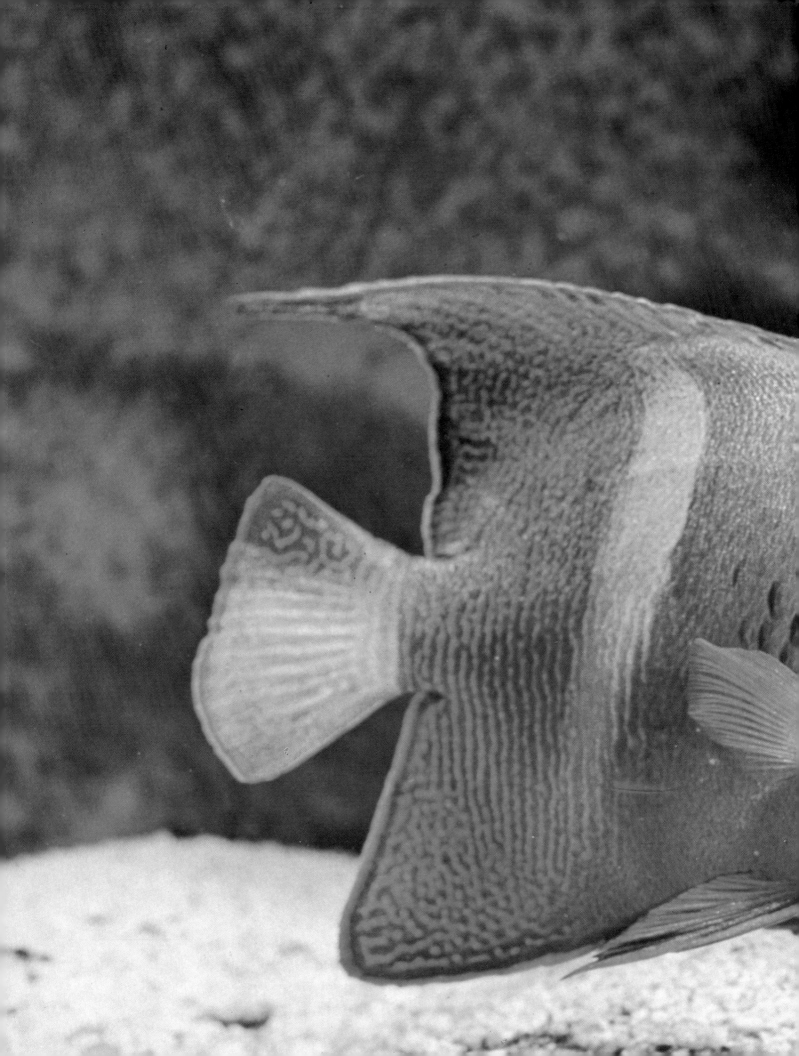

Fish

Fishes live in water
all the time. A fish breathes
underwater, through the gills
on the side of its body. A
fish's body is covered with
scales. It swims by waggling
its tail from side to side.
On a fish's back there are
one or more fins which help
to keep it upright in the water.
Near the fish's throat
there is a pair of fins, and
there is another pair of fins
at the base of its tail.
These also help it to balance,
and the fish uses them
to steer and brake. Left:
purple moon angelfish.
Below centre: Malayan
angelfish. Bottom: cardinal.

Flamingo

Flamingoes have lovely pink feathers. They live on lakes in many parts of the world. Flamingoes feed on tiny water plants and animals, which they scoop up in their crooked beaks.

Fly

Many insects which fly are called 'flies'. But true flies only have two wings. Flies are found everywhere in the world. Some are troublesome to man, because they spread disease.

Fossil

Fossil means 'a thing dug up'. Fossils are the remains of prehistoric animals and plants. They died many millions of years ago, and were buried in mud. More mud piled up on them, and gradually they turned into rock. Usually only the hard parts of the body, like bones and teeth, turn into fossils. The fossil in the picture is the shell of an ammonite, an animal which once lived in the sea.

Fox

Foxes belong to the dog family. There are several kinds of foxes, and they are found all over the world. This is the red fox. It has a reddish coat and a bushy tail, called a brush. All foxes have the same habits. During the day, they live in holes in the ground. At night they hunt small animals and birds. Baby foxes are called cubs. They are looked after by both the parents.

Frigate bird

The frigate bird is a seabird. It steals food from other birds.
It chases a bird and makes it drop its catch. Then the frigate bird
catches the food in mid-air. In the breeding season,
the male has a large scarlet pouch of skin on his breast
which he fills with air. He uses this to show off to the female.

Frog

Frogs spend part of their lives in water and part on dry land. They have a smooth, shiny skin, which is usually green or brown. Their back legs are much longer than their front legs, so they can move around easily in leaps and bounds.
Frogs breathe mostly through their moist skins. So even when they are on land, they must find a damp place to live in.

Left: green frog. Above: laughing frog. Below: cricket frog.

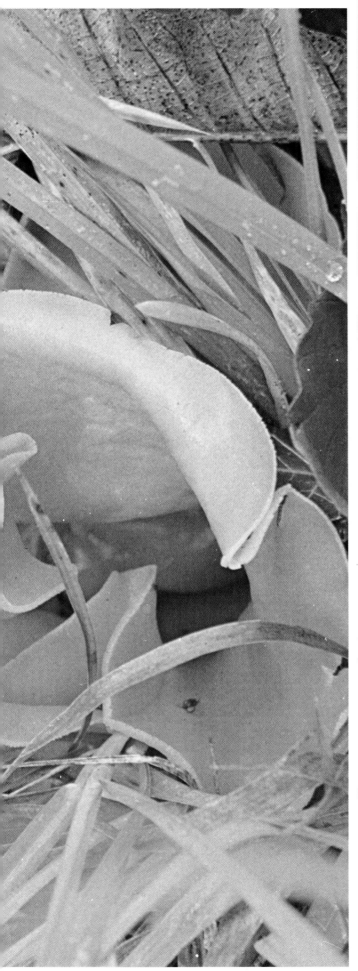

Fungi

Fungi are rather peculiar plants. Some are very, very small. Others are large and bulky, for example toadstools and mushrooms. Fungi grow best in warm, damp places. A fungus cannot make its own food from sunlight, like green plants. It has to take it from other plants or animals, on which it lives. Left: orange-peel fungus. Above: a type of grifolia fungus.

Gg

Gecko

Geckos are lizards. They are very common, and live in almost all the warm countries of the world. Some are quite small, others are as long as 35 centimetres. Geckos live in deserts, in trees or among rocks. Sometimes they come into people's houses, but they do no harm. A gecko has hooks on its toes, which help it to run up walls or cling upside down to ceilings.

Giraffe

The giraffe lives in Africa. It has very long legs and a very long neck. It also has short horns, which are bony knobs covered with skin. The giraffe is the tallest animal in the world. The baby giraffe is already as tall as a man when it is born. Because they are so tall, giraffes can stretch up and eat leaves off very high trees. Their coats are spotted, so they are difficult to see. This protects them from their enemies, such as lions.

Gnu

Gnus are rather clumsy-looking antelopes. They are also called wildebeestes. The gnu has smooth horns which curve outwards. It has long hair on its muzzle and throat, and a mane of hair on its back. Gnus live in large herds, which feed on the grassy plains of Africa. Soon after the calf is born, it is strong enough to run beside its mother.

Goat

Goats are first cousins to sheep. Both goats and sheep can climb easily over rocks. Goats climb even better than sheep. They often live in mountains. The mountain goat lives in the Rocky Mountains, on the steep mountain slopes. Even when it is only a few days old, it is sure-footed. It can climb among loose rocks, and it soon learns to leap from rock to rock. A young goat is called a kid. You can see a kid in the picture.

Goldfinch

The goldfinch is a
very pretty little bird.
It has a reddish-brown
back and black wings,
with a gold bar on
each wing. The gold bar
gives the bird its name.
The goldfinch has
a short beak. It eats
the seeds from pine and
birch trees, and seeds
from thistle heads.

Goldfish

Many years ago the Chinese took
some small green and brown fishes
from the rivers and kept them
as pets. Some of the fish were gold,
and these were specially bred for
their beautiful colour. The goldfish
many people keep today are descended
from those Chinese fishes.

Goose

A goose looks like a duck,
but it is bigger and it has
a long neck. It does not
quack like a duck, but it
makes a sound called a
'honk' instead. The male
goose is called a gander.
Geese feed on grass and
other plants. They spend
less time in water than
ducks. A baby goose
is called a gosling.

Gorilla

Gorillas are very big, black apes.
They live in Africa. Some gorillas
live in the wet forests, and some
live in the mountains. They walk
on all fours, with their knuckles
on the ground. They do not like
climbing trees. Gorillas eat fruit,
leaves, bark and roots. They live
in small groups. Although they look
fierce, they are peaceful animals.

Guinea pig

You may have had a guinea pig as a pet.
It is a rodent, or gnawing, animal,
with a round, stout body and no tail.
Wild guinea pigs live in dry, stony
country in South America. They eat
all kinds of grass and plants.
Guinea pigs are very timid animals.

Hamster

The hamster is a favourite pet. The most popular is this golden hamster, which has light, reddish-brown fur. Wild hamsters live on dry plains, or on the edges of deserts. They eat cereals, roots, leaves and fruit. Hamsters collect food in their large cheek pouches, and carry it back to their burrows.

Hare

The hare is very like a rabbit, but it has longer ears and longer legs. It can run very fast. It usually has reddish-brown fur, but in some cold countries the fur turns white in winter. The Arctic hare of the far north has white fur all the year round.

Hedgehog

The hedgehog has a coat of spines, which covers its back. When it is frightened, the hedgehog raises the spines, so that they stick up sharply. If the danger does not pass, the hedgehog rolls itself up in a ball. Hedgehogs sleep during the day. They come out at night to feed on worms, slugs and beetles. In cold countries, hedgehogs go to sleep for the winter.

Heron

Herons are birds with long legs, long necks and long bills.
They use these to catch fish and small water animals.
Most herons nest in colonies high up in trees or on cliffs.
Herons are found in many parts of the world, but most of them
live in warm countries. The Louisiana heron in the picture is
common in the salt marshes along the coast of North America.

Hibiscus

The hibiscus grows in warm countries. It may be a shrub or a small tree.
Its flowers are large, 10 centimetres or more across, with five petals. They are white,
yellow or red. The centre of the flower is red or purple. The hibiscus is often
grown in gardens because it is so beautiful.

Hippopotamus

The hippopotamus is an enormous animal. It has a very large body and short legs.
Its thick skin has no hairs, except for a few bristles. Hippos live in rivers
in Africa. They spend most of the day in the water, with only their ears, eyes
and nostrils showing. At night they come on land to feed on grass.

Holly

Holly is a very common shrub. It is an evergreen, which means it does not lose
all its leaves in winter. Usually the leaves of holly are prickly. In spring
the holly has very tiny white flowers, and from these grow bright red berries.

Honeysuckle

Honeysuckle grows on hedges or on the edges of woods. It twines
its way up the shrubs, and curls its slender stem around the branches for support.
Honeysuckle flowers grow in clusters. They have a very sweet scent. The scent
attracts moths to come to the honeysuckle and drink its nectar.

Horses

Horse

All the breeds of domestic horse we know today are descended from wild horses.
Most wild horses have now died out. The wild horse has an erect mane,
not drooping like that of the domestic horse. Horses were once used to pull coaches
and carriages, and soldiers rode on them to battle. Today some horses are still
used for farm work, but most of them are ridden for sport and pleasure.
Previous pages: wild Camargue horses. Left inset: Lusitano horse. Left:
Russian Akhal-Teké horse.

Hummingbird

Most of the beautiful little hummingbirds live in the forests of South America.
They have brightly coloured, shiny feathers. Their wings beat so fast
that they sound like the hum of a bee. Hummingbirds have long, narrow bills,
which they push into flowers to sip the nectar. They also eat small insects
and spiders. The hummingbird's nest is very tiny. It is made of moss
and spiders' webs.

Ii

Iguana

Iguanas are lizards. They live in warm parts of America.
Some live on the ground, others live in trees. Some are large, up to 1·8 metres long.
Most iguanas eat small animals, as well as plant food. The mother iguana
lays about 50 eggs deep down in sandy ground. The picture shows
a large iguana which lives on the Galapagos Islands in the Pacific Ocean.

Iris

The iris has large, beautiful flowers. They are white, yellow or purple-blue.
Each flower is at the top of a strong, erect stem. Sometimes there are two
or three flowers on one stem. The leaves of the iris are sword-shaped. Most irises
grow from an underground stem, called a rhizome. The name iris comes from
the Greek word for rainbow, because of the iris's beautiful colours.

Jj

Jay

The jay is a member of the crow family.
But instead of being black, like a crow,
it is coloured. The blue jay of North America
has more blue feathers than the European jay.
Jays live in woods. They eat all sorts
of seeds, fruits and insects. Sometimes
they steal the eggs of other birds.

Jellyfish

The jellyfish is a relative of the sea anemones and the corals. But instead of
staying in one place like them, it can swim about in the sea. Its body is made
of a substance which feels like jelly. Most jellyfishes are shaped like an umbrella
or a bell. Underneath this is the mouth, which is surrounded by tentacles.
Sometimes the tentacles have stinging cells, which the jellyfish uses to catch its prey.
The large jellyfish in the picture has small fishes swimming around it. These fish
live with the jellyfish because its stinging cells protect them from their enemies.

Kangaroo

The kangaroo lives in Australia. The largest kangaroo is as tall as a man. Kangaroos have strong hindlegs. Instead of running, they bound over the ground in long leaps. They have long tails, which help to balance them. Kangaroo babies are no bigger than a bean when they are born. The baby lives in a pouch on its mother's belly, until it is old enough to jump on its own.

Kestrel

The kestrel is a hunting bird. It hovers in the air,
watching for any small animals on the ground below.
When the kestrel sees an animal, it swoops down
very fast. It uses its strong claws to lift up the prey.

Kingfisher

There are many different kinds of kingfisher in the world.
This kingfisher lives in Europe, Asia and North Africa.
Its head and wings are a bright, shining blue-green,
and its breast is reddish-brown. Kingfishers feed on fishes.
They dive into a stream or river, and catch the fish
in their long bills. Kingfishers nest in holes in riverbanks.

Koala bear

The koala bear lives in Australia It is small and cuddly, and looks like a teddy bear. It has tufted ears, a black snout and a stumpy tail. Its fur is grey on the back and white underneath. The koala lives in the eucalyptus, or gum, trees. It eats the leaves and shoots of these trees. When the baby is born, the mother carries it in her pouch, like a kangaroo mother.

Kookaburra

The kookaburra lives in Australia, like the koala bear.
It is a kind of kingfisher, but it is not so colourful
and it does not live near streams. Instead it lives
in woods and gardens. It is well known for its loud,
laughing call. Another name for it is laughing jackass,
or 'Jackie' for short.

Ll

Ladybird

The ladybird is a very popular little beetle. Gardeners like it because it eats plant lice, which spoil the plants. You can see some plant lice in this picture. The ladybird's bright colours warn its enemies to keep away. This is because it is nasty to eat. In winter ladybirds go to sleep under the bark of trees.

Lily

The lily is a popular garden plant. It grows from a bulb. The picture shows a Madonna lily, which comes from the Balkans in south-east Europe. It also grows wild in other parts of Europe. The Romans carried lilies with them on their travels, and planted them. They used the bulb of the lily to make medicines to heal their wounds.

Lion

The lion is a very big cat. It has
a long, heavy body. Its thick fur
is golden brown. The male lion has
a thick black mane around its neck.
The female lion is called a lioness.
You can see her in the picture.
In the wild, lions live on the grassy plains
of Africa. They eat antelopés and zebras.
A lion runs very fast when it is hunting.
It can break the neck of a zebra
with one blow of its paw.

Lizard

Lizards are reptiles. They
have long bodies and tails.
Usually they have short legs.
Their bodies are covered by
small scales. Some lizards,
like the slow-worm, have
no legs. Most lizards live
in hot countries.

Llama

The llama lives in South America.
It is a kind of small camel,
but it has not got a hump.
Its long shaggy coat is sometimes
white, sometimes much darker.
The llama has been used
for thousands of years to carry
loads in the mountains. It is
  a very good climber.

Lupin

The lupin is a garden plant.
It is a member of the pea family.
Lupin flowers may be red, white,
yellow, blue or purple. The seeds
are in pods, like a pea. There are
also tree lupins, which are
larger plants with woody stems.

Maple

The maple is a tree which grows especially
in North America. At the end of the summer,
its leaves turn bright red or yellow,
and seeds fall from the tree. Maple sugar
and maple syrup come from the sap, or juice,
of the sugar maple.

Mineral

Rocks are made of minerals. Some minerals are joined together in a crystal formation. Many precious stones occur in this form. The picture shows an amethyst, which is a precious stone. The most common mineral is quartz. Sand contains many particles of quartz. Metal ores, asbestos and rock salt are also minerals. Many minerals dissolve in water, like salt. Living things need minerals to grow.

Mole

The mole lives underground. It does not often come to the surface. The mole tunnels through the soil, using the strong claws on its forefeet. As it digs its way through the earth, it finds worms, which it eats. When it makes its tunnels, the mole must scrape away the earth. It pushes the earth to the surface of the ground, where you can see it as molehills.

Monkey

Monkeys look very much like little men, except that they are covered with hair and have tails. They live in trees in warm countries. They swing from branch to branch. They grasp the branches with their hands, just like we do. They also grasp with their feet, which they use like another pair of hands. Some monkeys wrap their tails round the branches to help them hold on.

Moth

Moths are very like butterflies. They have two pairs of broad wings, which are covered with tiny scales. A moth spreads its wings when it settles on something, but a butterfly folds its wings over its back. Above: cinnabar moth. Left: Provence burnet moth.

Mouse

The mouse is a small, furry animal. It has a sharp nose, bright eyes, large ears
and a long tail. Mice feed mainly on seeds, but they also come into houses to live.
Indoors they will eat almost any kind of food. They sometimes do harm because they
gnaw holes in wood.

Mushroom

A mushroom is a kind of toadstool, which we can eat. Mushrooms grow wild in fields.
They are also grown on mushroom farms. Mushrooms grow wild at the end of summer,
especially when the weather is wet. The little white umbrella which you can see
in the picture is not the whole of the plant. The real plant is a mass
of white threads which grow in the ground beneath. The umbrella part carries the seeds
for future mushrooms.

Nn

Narcissus

The narcissus grows from a bulb. In the spring, the bulb sends up a stem and leaves, and a flower grows. After the flower has been pollinated, it turns into a pod of seeds. Eventually the stem and leaves die back into the bulb. A daffodil is a kind of narcissus. The picture shows a poet's narcissus. It is also called a pheasant's eye.

Newt

Like frogs, newts spend part of their lives in water and part on land.
They have long slender bodies and flattened tails. The upper parts
of most newts are dark grey or brown, sometimes with spots or streaks.
The undersides are usually brightly coloured in orange, red or yellow.
The picture shows a male crested newt. In the breeding season,
he grows a crest down his back.

Octopus

The octopus lives in the sea. It has a soft body, with eight long arms around its mouth. The arms are lined with suckers. When the octopus wants to move on the sea bed, it creeps along on its arms. It uses the suckers to grip. An octopus can swim swiftly, either backwards or forwards.

Opossum

The opossum is an animal which carries its baby
in its pouch, like a kangaroo. It looks like
a very big rat. The opossum lives in woods in America.
It stays mainly on the ground, but sometimes it climbs
trees. When an opossum is frightened, it pretends
to be dead, so that its enemies will go away.

Orang-utan

The orang-utan is a large ape which lives in the jungles of Borneo. Its name means
'old man of the woods'. The orang-utan's body is covered with long, brownish-red hair.
It has very long arms, which it uses to swing through the trees. On the ground
it uses its arms like crutches. It eats leaves, fruit, insects and birds' eggs.

Orchid

Orchids are some of the most beautiful
flowers in the world. There are many
different kinds. The best of them grow
in the hot, wet forests of tropical
countries. Some orchids also grow in
colder countries. These orchids usually
have very small flowers. They are not
easy to find, because they grow hidden
in the grass. The picture shows
the purple heath orchid.

Osprey

The osprey is a large hunting bird,
which feeds mainly on fish.
It spends most of its time
flying over the sea, or over
a lake or river, looking for fish.
When the osprey sees a fish,
it plunges onto the water.
It grasps the fish in its claws,
and then flies to a perch to eat it.
It hardly ever misses.

Ostrich

The ostrich is the largest living bird.
A large male ostrich may be as tall
as 2.5 metres. It has a very long neck
and long legs. The male ostrich has
beautiful black and white feathers,
but the female's feathers are brown.
Although the ostrich can run very fast,
it cannot fly. In the past, many ostriches
were killed for their white feathers.
Today they live wild only in East Africa.

Otter

Otters spend most of their time in rivers. Their hind feet are large and webbed, to help them swim. Their broad tails are also used for swimming. Otters are very good swimmers, but they can also run fast on land. They feed on fishes, birds and small animals. You do not see otters often, because they are very shy. They are very playful and enjoy tobogganing in the snow.

Owl

Owls are birds which hunt their prey at night. They eat small animals, such as mice and voles. They have large eyes that can see well even in dim light. Owls fly very quietly, so that their prey cannot hear them. They also have very sharp hearing. They can catch a mouse on a very dark night if it makes only a slight noise. Most owls are dull brown so you do not often see them, but you hear their loud hoots and screams.

Pp

Panda

Ever since the panda was first
shown in zoos, it has been
very popular with children.
It has a cuddly body,
with thick, black-and-white fur.
Outside zoos, pandas are very rare.
They live in bamboo forests
in the mountain country of China.
Pandas feed on bamboo shoots
and other plants, as well as
small animals. They sit upright
and hold their food in their hands.

Pansy

The most famous member of the Violet family is the wild pansy, or heartsease. The pansy grows wild in Europe, but many garden varieties have been bred from it. A pansy flower has five petals, in three colours. There are lines on the lower three petals, which make the flower look like a little face.

Parrot

Parrots are birds which live in tropical forests. These two parrots live in South America. Most parrots are brightly coloured. They have large heads, strong, hooked beaks and strong claws on their toes. Unlike any other birds, they can use their feet as 'hands' to hold their food. Parrots are kept as pets. Some are very popular pets, because they imitate people talking. Turn the page for pictures of different kinds of parrots. This page: scarlet macaws. Following page left: scarlet crested cockatoo. Following page right: eastern rosella.

Peacock

The peacock is the male of the peafowl. It is one of the most beautiful birds in the world. It is famous for its long train of feathers, which are decorated with spots like eyes. Peafowl feed on the ground on seeds, fruit and insects. At night they roost in the trees. They have a loud, screeching call.

Pelican
The pelican is a very odd bird. What makes it look so odd is
its enormous bill. The lower part of the bill
has a pouch, which can hold nearly 10 litres
of water. The pelican feeds on fishes.
It uses the pouch like a net.

Penguin
The penguin is a seabird. It lives
in very cold lands. The penguin cannot fly.
It waddles around upright on its very short legs.
It is a good swimmer, and it feeds
on fishes. The largest penguins in the world
are the emperor penguins of Antarctica.
You can see them in the picture. The female
lays only one egg. The parents take it in turn
to hold the egg on their feet, to keep it warm
until it hatches.

Periwinkle

The periwinkle is a kind of sea snail.
It looks rather like a garden snail,
but it is smaller. The flat periwinkles
in the picture are usually bright yellow.
Sometimes they are brown and black,
or orange and black. These periwinkles
live on the seashore. They eat seaweed.

Pig

The pig is a domestic animal which
is reared for its meat. The wild pig
is called a wild boar. The pig has
a heavy body and cloven, or divided,
hooves. It has a large snout, which
it uses to dig into the earth for food.
The female pig is called a sow.

Pigeon

Pigeons have beautiful cooing voices. Small pigeons are called doves. Pigeons and doves both have soft feathers which are grey, brown or pink. Some pigeons in hot countries have very bright colours. Pigeons feed on seeds and vegetables. People used to keep pigeons to carry messages. They are very common birds in large towns and cities.

Plankton

Animals which live in the sea must, like land animals,
feed either on plants or on other animals which have fed
on plants. Most of the plant food in the sea comes from
what is called plant plankton. This is made up
of millions and millions of very tiny, floating plants.
You need a microscope to see one plant, but in some places
there are so many of them that they colour the sea green.

Polar bear

The polar bear lives among the ice and snow
of the Arctic. It has hairy soles on its feet,
so that it can grip well on slippery ice.
It feeds on seals, seabirds and fish. It dives
and swims well. Sometimes it swims a long way
out to sea.

Pony

A pony is a small horse. It is up to 14½ hands high. A hand is a special measurement, which we use to measure horses and ponies. It is the same as 4 inches or 10 centimetres. Ponies are small, because they live in wild places where there is not much grass for them to eat. They are very hardy and nimble. There are many different breeds of pony. The picture shows an Icelandic pony, which lives in very cold conditions.

Poppy

There are wild poppies and garden poppies. All have beautiful flowers, with silky petals. In the middle of the flower is a seed box. As the petals fall, the seed box grows larger. You can shake the seed box like a pepper pot, and all the seeds will fall out.

Puffin

The puffin is a sea bird. It lives on the coasts around the North Atlantic. The puffin has a large, bright bill. During the breeding season, the bill looks even larger and becomes red, yellow and blue. The puffin lays one egg in a burrow at the top of a cliff. It feeds its chicks on fish.

Quail

The quail is a small bird with a short tail and short legs. The painted quail in the picture is only about the size of a sparrow. There are a hundred different kinds of quail. Most are brown. Quails live in families in open fields or pastures. When they make their nests, they just scrape the ground and line it with bits of grass.

Quetzal

The quetzal is one of the most beautiful birds in the world. It lives in the wet forests of central America. The male has a very long tail. It is three times as long as the rest of the bird. Quetzals nest in hollow trees. The male helps the female to incubate the eggs.

Rr

Rabbit

The rabbit has long ears and big eyes on the sides of its head. It has long hind legs, so it can run fast in leaps and bounds. As it runs, its short white tail bobs up and down. Rabbits dig their homes, called burrows, with their short front legs. The male rabbit is called a buck. The female is called a doe. Her babies are born blind and without fur.

Raccoon

The raccoon lives in North America.
It has dark marks on its face,
like a highwayman's mask.
Raccoons live near water.
They hunt small animals on land
or in the water. They catch
their prey with their front paws,
which are almost like hands.
Raccoons sometimes dip
their food in the water.

Redwood

The redwoods are some of the
tallest trees in the world.
They are a kind of pine tree.
They are called redwood
because of their red-brown bark.
Redwoods grow in North America.
Some live over 2,000 years.
The tallest of them is over
40 metres high.

Reindeer

The reindeer is a kind of deer. It lives in northern countries, where it is very cold. The reindeer is very hardy. Its hoofs are splayed so that it can run across the snow without sinking in. The people who live in Lapland have domesticated reindeer. They use reindeers as beasts of burden, and to give milk. Unlike other deer, both male and female reindeer have antlers.

Rhinoceros

There are five kinds of rhinoceros.
The best-known kinds live in India
and Africa. All have heavy bodies
and short, strong legs. A rhinoceros
has one or two curved horns on
its snout. The horns are made of hair
and not of bone, but they are
very hard. The rhinoceros has
a tough skin, and very little hair.
It looks as if it is wearing armour.
Although the rhinoceros is so large,
it only eats grass and leaves.

Robin

The robin redbreast in the
picture is one of Britain's
most popular birds. It sings
in the winter when most birds
are silent, and it is often
very tame. The robin feeds
in gardens and parks
on worms and insects. The robin
of North America also has
a red breast, but it is larger
and is really a kind of thrush.
Other red-breasted birds,
which are also called robins,
live in India and Australia.

Rose

Roses have been grown in gardens
for at least 2,000 years.
They are very beautiful,
and have a wonderful scent.
Rose petals are used
to make perfumes. The stems
of the flowers have
sharp thorns, so they are
difficult to pick.

Salamander

The salamander, like frogs and toads, spends part of its life in water and part on land. So it is an amphibian. It has a long body, with a long tail and weak legs. Most salamanders lay their eggs in water, but some give birth to live babies. The babies look like the parents, but they are very much smaller.

Seagull

The seagull is a common seabird. It lives on the coast, and never goes very far out to sea. Seagulls often follow ships, looking for food which is thrown overboard. Many seagulls live in towns, where they eat food on rubbish dumps. Seagulls are usually white, with some black on their wings. Some of them have a black back, or a black head. They like to feed on fish, but they will eat almost anything.

Sea horse

A sea horse is a small fish which swims upright. Its head is like a tiny horse's head. It drives itself through the water with a fin on its back. A sea horse looks like a chesspiece, except for its long tail. It coils its tail round seaweed to anchor itself. The female sea horse lays her eggs in a pouch on the male's belly. So the father has to look after the babies.

Sea lion

The sea lion is a kind of seal. You may have seen one in a zoo or circus,
where they are very popular. Sea lions have longer necks than other
seals. They can swing their hindlegs forwards, and use them for walking.
Sea lions perform tricks in circuses. They walk, and they can also
balance balls on their noses.

Sea slug

The slugs which live in gardens are not very beautiful. But the slugs
which live in the sea are pretty, as you can see in the picture.
Sea slugs feed on small sea animals, which are second cousins
to sea anemones. The bodies of these small animals have large numbers
of stinging cells, but this does not worry the sea slugs. They can
even eat animals which sting.

Sea urchin

Sea urchins are related to starfishes. But instead of having
a star-shaped body, they are round and covered with spines. The old name
for the hedgehog was urchin, so because sea urchins are spiny like
a hedgehog, they are called by the same name. A sea urchin's mouth
is on its underside. It has five teeth, which it uses to chew seaweed.

Seaweed

Seaweeds grow on the seashore, where there are rocks which they can hold onto.
Some seaweeds are very large, but all seaweeds are very simple plants. They
do not have flowers, and they do not have a real stem, or leaves, or a root.
Instead, they have what we call fronds. Seaweeds may be green, brown or red.
The picture shows several different seaweeds.

Shark

The shark is a very fierce fish. It has a pointed nose and sharp teeth.
Sharks feed on other animals in the sea, such as other fishes. The largest shark
is the whale shark. It is 16 metres long, but its teeth are tiny and it feeds
on tiny animals. The man-eater shark is 10 metres long. Sometimes
it attacks people swimming. It can even kill them, but this is very rare.

Sheep

Sheep are important to man, because
they have woolly coats. Sheep are kept
on farms. Each year their wool is cut off,
or sheared. The wool is used to make
our clothes. The male sheep is called
a ram. The female sheep is called a ewe.
Each year lambs are born. which are able
to walk soon after their birth.

Shell

Many animals which live in the sea
have shells. The shells protect them
from their enemies, and also from
the waves on the shore. Some shells
are coiled in a spiral, like the periwinkle
and the whelk shell. Most shells
are in two parts, like the mussel and
the oyster. The parts are hinged so that
they open like a book. Shells are made
of lime, which the animals take from
the sea water. Crabs also have shells.

Skunk

The skunk lives in North America. To defend
itself, it gives off a very nasty smell.
This smell comes from a liquid which the skunk
can squirt out from under its tail. Its fur
is black and white, so it is easy to see.
This warns other animals to keep away from it.

Slow-worm

The slow-worm is a lizard which has no legs.
It has a long body and long tail. It looks
like a large worm, except that it is covered
with scales. A slow-worm has to wriggle

Snail

A snail has a very soft body.
It would soon dry up and die if
it was left in the sun and wind,
so it carries a hard shell around
with it. The shell also helps
to protect it, but many animals
still eat snails. Wherever
it goes, a snail leaves a trail
of silvery slime. This helps it
to crawl over loose dust or earth.
Snails feed on small plants. They
tear the leaves into tiny pieces
with their file-like tongues.

over the ground, like a snake. It spends
most of its time in the earth, and feeds on slugs.
On warm days, it likes to lie in the sun.

Snowdrop

The white snowdrop flowers bloom in winter,
when the trees are bare. They are the first
flowers of the new year. Often snowdrops
have to grow up through the snow to bloom.
Their flowers are shaped like small, white bells.

Sparrow

Almost as soon as people began to grow crops and build houses, this sparrow came to live with them. So it was called the house sparrow. It does not have bright colours or a sweet song, like many other birds. But it is popular, because it is so cheeky and gay.

Spider

People sometimes call spiders insects, but they are different. An insect has three parts to its body, but a spider only has two. An insect has three pairs of legs, but a spider has four pairs. Spiders feed on insects. Many spiders spin a web, which traps the insects. Often the female spider makes a bag, in which she lays her eggs.

Squid

The squid is related to the octopus. But
instead of being round, like an octopus,
it is torpedo-shaped, and instead of having
eight arms, it has ten. Eight of its arms are
of medium length and two are very long.
These two arms are called tentacles. The squid
uses its tentacles to seize its prey. Some squid
are very small, only the size of a finger.
The largest squid is 18 metres long. It is called
the giant squid and lives deep in the oceans.

Squirrel

A squirrel is a rodent, or gnawing animal.
Most squirrels live in trees. They are
very good climbers, and they can jump
from branch to branch. They have bushy tails,
which act as balancers. Some squirrels
stay on the ground, and live in burrows.
The chipmunk is a ground squirrel. The picture
shows a grey squirrel, which lives in trees.

Starfish

The common starfish has five arms, and so it looks like a star. It is sometimes called a sea star. Some starfish have many more than five arms. Underneath each arm, there are rows of hundreds of tiny suckers. These are called tube-feet. The starfish pulls itself along with these feet. Some starfish feed on mussels and oysters.

Swallow

The swallow is a small, blue bird, with a forked tail. It flies very fast, and snaps up insects in the air. Swallows spend the summer in North America, Europe and Asia. In the winter they fly south to warmer countries, such as South America, South Africa, Sri Lanka and Australia. Swallows make a nest of mud and dry grass in barns and other buildings.

Swan

Swans are large, long-necked water birds. The most familiar swan is the mute swan, which lives on rivers and lakes in many parts of the world. Its feathers are all white, and its bill, or beak, is orange, with a black knob on top. The black swan in the picture lives in Australia. It is all black, except for a few white wing feathers and a red bill. Swans are strong fliers, but they need a long stretch of water from which to take off. They feed mainly on water plants.

Tt

Tadpole

A baby frog is called a tadpole.
Its head and body are in one
piece and it has a long tail.
It swims by wriggling its tail.
At first a tadpole has no legs.
Then a pair of hind legs grow.
Later a pair of front legs
grow out. After this has
happened, the tadpole's
tail shrinks until there is
nothing left of it.
The tadpole has then
changed into a froglet.

Termite

Termites are insects which
live in warm countries.
They live in large colonies.
Some termites live under
the ground. Others build
huge mounds of earth.
Sometimes these mounds
are 2 metres high. Each
colony has a queen.
She has a very large body.
She lays millions of eggs.
Some termites are 'workers',
some are 'soldiers'.
The soldiers guard the
workers.

Thistle

The thistle belongs to the daisy family. This means that
each head of flowers is not a single bloom, but a collection
of many tiny flowers. These are called florets. When
the flowers of the thistle are dead, the seeds ripen. From
each floret there comes a seed with long silky fibres,
called thistledown. The wind catches the thistledown
and carries the seed away. All thistles have spiky leaves,
which hurt your hands if you try to pick them.

Tiger

Tigers live in Asia. They are one of the largest members
of the cat family. Tigers are slightly larger than lions.
Each tiger lives on its own, except in the breeding season
when two tigers pair up for a short while. Tigers feed
on animals, such as deer. To catch their prey, they stalk them
through the grass and then pounce on them suddenly. Tigers
use their strong claws and powerful teeth to kill their prey.

Toad

Toads are like frogs, but they have
drier skins and they do not hop.
In April and May, the female toad
lays two long strings of egg spawn.
Each string may contain as many as
10,000 eggs. In the breeding season,
the male toad makes a trilling croak.
The picture shows a green toad.

Tortoise

The tortoise has a very hard shell.
When it is frightened, it disappears
inside the shell to hide. The tortoise
walks very, very slowly. The picture
shows a giant tortoise. It grows
to more than 1 metre long.
Tortoises live a very long time,
sometimes over 100 years.

Toucan

The toucan is a large bird which lives in tropical America. It has a huge bill, which is sometimes as large as the bird itself. Toucans live in small flocks in the forests. They feed on fruit. Toucans make playful pets. They are good mimics, like parrots.

Turtle

The turtle is a reptile with a bony shell. Some turtles live on land, some live in the sea, and others live in rivers and streams. But all turtles have to come on land to lay their eggs. Some of the turtles which live in the sea are very large. Sometimes they weigh as much as 1 tonne. Others are much smaller. The turtle in the picture lives in North America.

Uu Vv

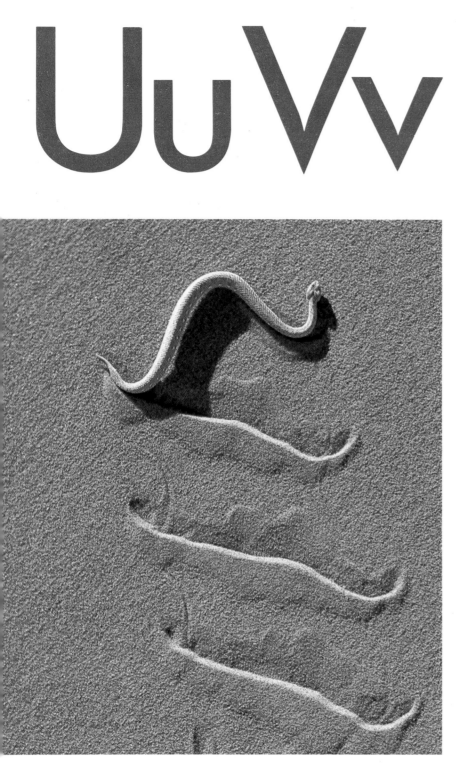

Viper

Some small poisonous snakes are called vipers.
One of these is the adder, which is found
in Europe. The adder has a V-mark on its head,
which helps us to remember the name, viper.
There are many kinds of vipers. The one
in the picture lives in deserts. It is not easy
for any animal to move quickly over sand, because
the sand gives way beneath it. This viper
jumps sideways. It has to coil and wind
its body to move. So it is called a sidewinder.

Vole

Voles are small, furry animals.
They look like mice. You can
tell the difference between
a vole and a mouse, because
a vole does not have large ears,
its eyes are small and hidden
in its fur, and its nose is blunt.
Most voles are not much bigger

than a house mouse, but the
water vole is as large as a rat.
You can see a baby water vole
in the picture.

Vulture

The vulture is a bird like
an eagle. It lives in
warm countries. A vulture
has a bare head and bare neck.
It feeds on the dead bodies
of large animals. The vulture
soars high up in the sky.
When a large animal dies,
the vulture flies down and eats
its flesh, leaving only the bones.
So it keeps the ground clean.

Ww

Warthog

The warthog is a kind of wild pig. It lives in Africa. The picture shows a mother warthog and her piglets. If an enemy threatens her piglets, she will fight to save them. She uses her sharp tusks as weapons.

Wallaby

A wallaby is a small kangaroo. It has long hind legs and short front legs. A wallaby hops instead of walking. It uses its long tail to balance. When it is resting, a wallaby sits upright and uses its tail to support itself. The mother wallaby carries her baby in a pouch on her belly. Wallabies live in Australia.

Wasp

Some wasps live in colonies, like honeybees. But, instead of making their combs of wax, the wasps make them of paper. The worker wasp settles on a post or a wooden tree trunk. It chews off tiny pieces of wood. The wasp wets the wood with saliva, and then goes on chewing until the wood turns into paper. This picture shows a paper wasps' nest in South Africa.

Waterlily

Waterlilies have their roots in the mud of ponds, lakes and slow-flowing rivers. Sometimes they completely cover the surface of the water. Their stems reach up to the surface so that the leaves float on the water. They have beautiful flowers, which are also on long stems that reach up to the surface. The largest waterlily is found in South America. It has leaves which are 2 metres across.

Whale

Although the whale lives in the sea and looks like a large fish, it is a mammal. It is warm-blooded, not cold-blooded like a fish. The whale's body is shaped like a fish, but its tail is flat. Whales swim by moving their tails up and down. The whale's nostrils form a blowhole on top of its head. Every so often the whale must come to the surface of the water to breathe through its blowhole. Some whales eat fish. Other whales eat small animals, like shrimps. Whales have always been hunted by man for their valuable oil.

Wheat

Our daily bread is made from flour, and flour is ground from grains of wheat. Wheat is the most important food crop for many people in the world The plant has long, sword-like leaves and tall stems, which have 'ears' at the top. Each ear is made up of grains, or seeds. Wheat is really only a wild grass, which has been domesticated and made to grow bigger seeds.

Wild boar

Years ago all pigs were wild. Some are still wild, but many more live on farms. A wild pig is called a wild boar. It has a coat of dark bristles. It also has tusks to defend itself. Baby wild boars have long stripes of white and brown.

Willow

Willows are trees with narrow leaves, which are often pointed. They grow best in damp ground near water. You often see them growing on river banks. Willows have catkins instead of flowers. One kind of willow has yellow or silver catkins. It is called a pussy willow, because the catkins look as if they are covered with fur.

Woodpecker

There are many kinds of woodpecker.
Most of them live in woods and forests.
They all have strong beaks, which
they use to dig into the bark of trees
to find insects or grubs to eat.
Woodpeckers run quickly up tree trunks,
using their short tails to help them
balance. They nest in holes, which
they chisel in the trees. The picture
shows the green woodpecker, which lives
in Europe.

Worm

There are many different sorts of worm. You
may have seen an earthworm in your garden, or
a lugworm at the seaside. Worms live underground.
They eat the soil, which contains decaying plants.
When they have eaten the food in the soil, they push
the empty soil to the surface of the ground. It makes
a worm cast. You can see a worm cast in the picture.

Wren

The wren is a small, dumpy bird with an upturned tail.
It feeds on insects and spiders, which it finds
under bushes. Wrens have a beautiful song. It is
so loud that the wren has been called the little bird
with the big voice. Its nest is a hollow ball.

Xx Yy Zz

Yew

The yew is an evergreen tree. This means that it keeps its leaves all the year.
The leaves are small, almost like pine needles. Some yew trees are male.
In spring the male trees are covered with tiny yellow catkins. At the end of the summer,
the female yew trees have red berries. Yews live hundreds of years. Their wood
is very hard. In the Middle Ages, yew wood was used to make longbows. Yew leaves
are poisonous to farm animals.

Zebra

The zebra is a striped horse. It is white with black or brown stripes.
Years ago, zebras lived in large herds on the African plains. When they are hunted
by lions, zebras usually run away. If a zebra does stand and fight, it kicks
with its hind feet and may drive the lion away. This young zebra was able
to run an hour after it was born.

Acknowledgments

The publishers would like to thank the following organizations and individuals for their kind permission to reproduce the photographs in this book:

AFA Colour Library Ltd. (Don McCaskill) 85 above, (E. H. Herbert) 113, 140; Afsen 33 below; Ardea 104, 151 above, (D. Avon & T. Tilford) 109, 118, (R. J. C. Blewitt) 157 above, (D. Burgess) 82, (Collet) 100 below, (P. Germain) 7 below, 126 below, (J. Marchington) 68, (W. Weisser) 79; A–Z Botanical Collection Ltd. 75, 106, 143; Douglass Baglin 84; Barnaby's Picture Library 90–91, 144; Bavaria Verlag 28 left, 114–115; Biofotos 4 & 10 left, 18, 36, 37, 83, 127, 128, 130, 156 above, 158; Bruce Coleman Ltd. 9 & 66–67, 10–11, 31 below, 56 above, 66–67, 74 below, 111 below, (J. & D. Bartlett) 16 below, 59, (S. C. Bisserot) 15, 94 below, (J. Burton) 14 right, 35, 41, 54–55, 69 below, 71 above, 94 above, 112 above, 129 left, 134 above right, 139 above and below, 148–149; (R. Campbell) 21, (F. Erize) 91 above, (J. Foott) 16 above, (P. Hinchliffe) 120, (D. Hughes) 142 above, (L. Lee Rue) 66, 100 above, (J. Markham) 136, 149, (N. Myers) 106–107, (G. Pizzey) 150, (M. Quarishy) 32, (H. Reinhard) 40, (N. Tomalin) 119; Colour Library International 13, 39, 46, 64–65, 111 above, 141; Tony Evans 102 left, 152; Fisons Ltd. 154–155; F. P. G. Inc. New York 28–29; Robert Gooden (Worldwide Butterflies) 6 below & 23 above, 30, endpapers; Sonia Halliday 24; Robert Harding Associates 116; David P. Healey 90; Eric Hosking 85 below, 110, 147; Institute of Geological Science 57; Jacana 14 left, 121, (P. du Pont) 33 above, (M. Kalifa) 25, (W. Schraml) 153, (J. Varin) 58, (A. Visage) 8 & 49 below; Leslie Johns 125; Frank Lane 48, 87, (A. Christiansen) 102 right, (N. Duerden) 52, (H. Schrempp) 105; Moorfield Aquatics 55 above & below, 67; Natural Science Photos 95, 124 above, (J. N. Wood) 7 above & 61 below; NHPA 35, (H. R. Allen) 62, 62–63, 88, (A. M. Anderson) 38 above, (A. Bannister) 12, 19, 31 above, 34 above, 46–47, 49 above, 89, 142 below, 148, 151 below, (F. Blackburn) 20 above, 157 below, (K. Blackburn) 124 below, (J. B. Blossom) 96, 107, 146, (J. M. Clayton) 132–133, (S. Dalton) 60–61, 72, 98, 117 right, 126 above, (E. K. Degginger) 92, (B. Hawkes) 122–123, (G. Hyde) 50, 97, (L. Jackman) 156–157, (P. Johnson) 64 below, (A. Mitchell) 122 left, (L. H. Newman) 20 below, (K. B. Newman) 103, (L. Perkins) 61 above, 134 centre left, 145 above, (R. Perry) 80, (G. Pizzey) 38 below, 108, (I. Polunin) 73, (M. Savonius) 91 below, (T. Stack) 11 right, 5 & 117 left, (J. Tallon) 44, 53, (M. W. F. Tweedie) 17, 23 below, 56 below, 94 below, (L. B. Williamson) 145 below; Tierbilder Okapia 101; Photo Aquatics (Ben Cropp) 131, (Herman Gruhl) 129 right; Picturepoint Ltd. 50–51, 74 above; Popperfoto 69 above, 159; Rapho 76–77; John Rigby 45; Seaphot (P. M. David) 6 above, 138, (John Lythgoe) 34 below; Harry Smith Horticultural Photographic Collection 81, 99, 134 below right; Spectrum Colour Library 1; Tony Stone Associates 27, 154; Sally Anne Thompson (Animal Photography) 26, 42–43 above & below, 43, 78 above & below; M. W. F. Tweedie 137; Douglas P. Wilson 114; ZEFA 42 left, 65, 70, 71 below, 86–87, 112 below, (Damm) 132, (Hartmann Studio) 92–93.

First published in Great Britain by Sundial Books Limited
This edition published by Treasure Press
59 Grosvenor Street
London W1

© 1976 Hennerwood Publications
Reprinted 1984
ISBN 0 907407 40 4
Printed in Hong Kong